The Adventures of Lala and her Papa

MW01296743

We dedicate this book to
life's most valuable love…
family.

Lala's Papa had spent a'lotta time
going from Alaska to Nebraska,
Iceland to New Zealand,
and all around the world.
With his camera in tow,
he was always ready to GO!

1

AUSTRALIA

ISRAEL

2

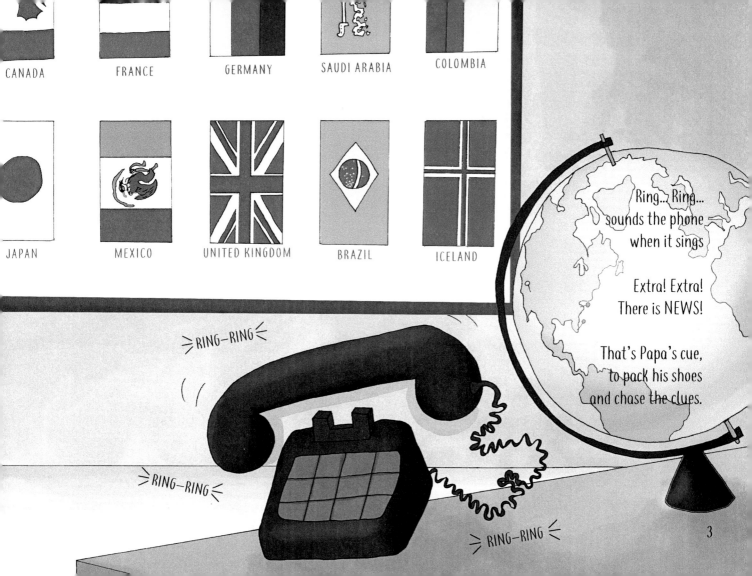

CANADA

FRANCE

GERMANY

SAUDI ARABIA

COLOMBIA

JAPAN

MEXICO

UNITED KINGDOM

BRAZIL

ICELAND

Ring... Ring...
sounds the phone
when it sings

Extra! Extra!
There is NEWS!

That's Papa's cue,
to pack his shoes
and chase the clues.

RING-RING

RING-RING

RING-RING

3

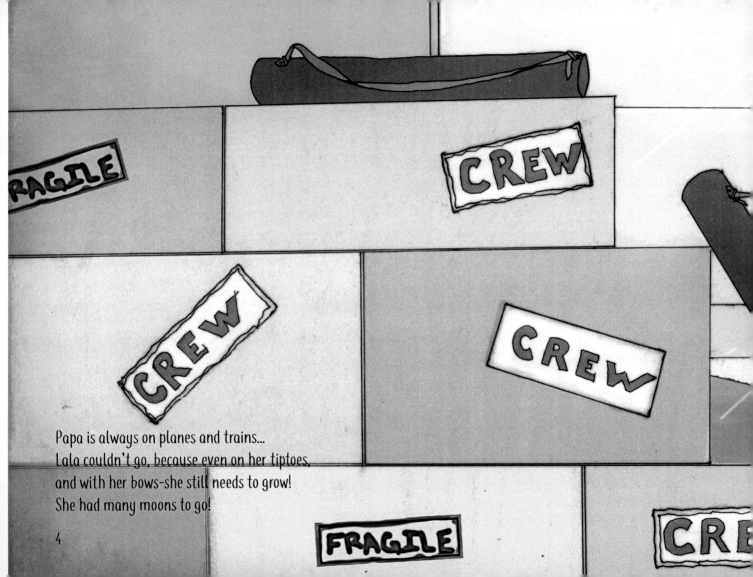

Papa is always on planes and trains...
Lala couldn't go, because even on her tiptoes,
and with her bows-she still needs to grow!
She had many moons to go!

4

Papa sets-up the stage,
to report the NEWS, that was all the rage.
There are grips for gripping,
sound to be wound abound,
lights to help capture the pictures,
and always QUIET on Papa's set—
SHHHHHHH!

5

Lala is happy when her Papi comes home in a snappy.
He always drags home bags of treats
from every different country!

Yippeeee for the teas,
which are a fancy 'oui' from overseas!

6

On days when Papa edits videos,
he always lets Lala have a sneak peek!
He's won tons and tons of awards...
but a little birdie told me, he ain't got nothin' on me!

7

TICK-TOCK

TICK-TOCK

After school, Lala waits for her Papa
cuz' he saves his stories
for her inventories!

Tick' Tock goes the clock —
And there is a Honk, Honk, Honk...
Papa's car is back on the block!

8

Lala fumbles, stumbles and tumbles
to give him a huggles—
and he just chuckles,
cuz' that's just the way this cookie crumbles!

9

Sometimes Papa shuffles upon scuffles...
Oftentimes, he flies high in the sky for an eagle's eye;
Other times, he rides side-by-side with a camel's stride!

Step inside our ride,
let's go far and wide,
for an adventure that's sure
to leave you starry-eyed!

11

Papa had to take the show on the road...
he was so upbeat to be in the Mid East,
where he took a ride on a leashed beast.

Click, Clock— Tick, Tock—
Plick, Pluck— Cackle and Crackle,
hackled the knees of the camel.

The camel's rumble made
Papa's tummy scrumble!
The bumps from the humps
thumped like loud drums —
and the funky skunky jelly,
from the camel's belly was so smelly!

12

Camel School

"tap"

What a treat, Lala went to greet Papa,
back home from his desert quest.
Papa took a beat, and said:
"These camels' drool is not cool, they need to go to school!"

"Lala, teach the camels to brush their teeth,
because of the heat, they smell like dirty feet!
You would turn red as a beet, when their fleas cause you to sneeze!"

13

In the blink of an eye, Papa was back in the sky!
He's always in the know and ready to Go, Go, Go!

14

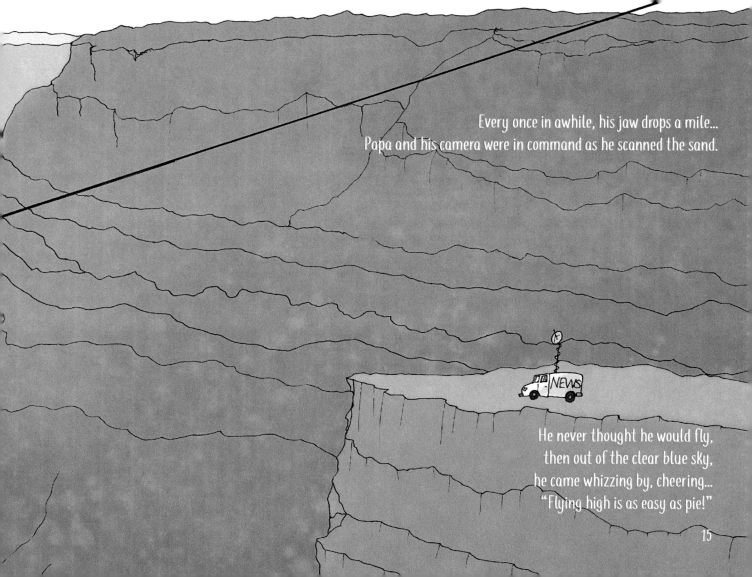

Every once in awhile, his jaw drops a mile...
Papa and his camera were in command as he scanned the sand.

He never thought he would fly,
then out of the clear blue sky,
he came whizzing by, cheering...
"Flying high is as easy as pie!"

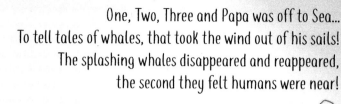

One, Two, Three and Papa was off to Sea...
To tell tales of whales, that took the wind out of his sails!
The splashing whales disappeared and reappeared,
the second they felt humans were near!

The whales had a song, that was so strong,
so Papa played along to the dinggggs and donggggs of
the very loooong song!

17

Papa's eye was the key to the world's TV...
He would soon be able to film thousands of the finest athletes compete.

From the jumping and flipping of the gymnasts
to the cheering from the dipping and kicking in swimming...
The games bring about your desire for winning.

South Korea to Atlanta, Vancouver to London—
whether it's Summer or Winter,
they are the hall of fame of athletic games!

It's not the same, with any other game.
Here any defeat, is NEVER a conceit...
it's the purest of treats, just to compete!

Next thing you Know,
Papa was in the snow, within a stone's throw,
from a volcano!

With his camera in tow, all systems were a go...
Who needs a drone, when Papa can get flown into the cone?

In Iceland, he saw tons of ice stones thrown from the danger zone.

Didn't you know... Papa is crazy to the bone!

It was a free light show and quite a bright glow,
that could excite anyone's fright!

Before you know, Papa was off to another show...
Wearing lots of clothes,
because it blowed busloads of snows!

It was quite dark up in the Arctic—
where there were only comets soaring like rockets.

In the Tundra...
no one could outrun the fast ones,
they even make your hair
stand in the air!

Oh, those Polar Bears!

I bet you didn't know...
they are NOT as white as snow,
but even so — they steal the show!

Remember to lay low and walk REALLY slow
or just tip toe, because these beasts from the snow
don't like to be shadowed!

Papa says, they are very touch and go!

23

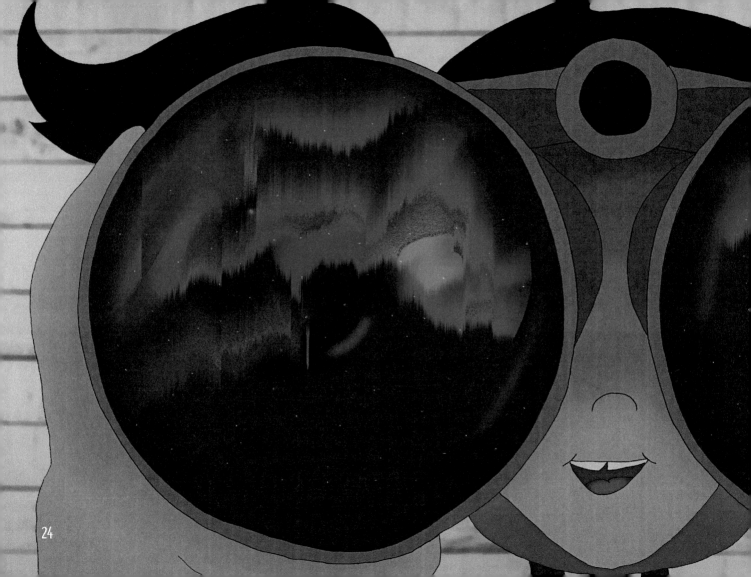

When Papa was with the Polar Bears,
he had to stop and stare
at the colorful lights in the sky,
which were so bright.

The Northern Lights were a sure sight...
like a trillion stoplights.

Charged particles from Earth and the Sun,
collide in a rainbow of glow.
From mellow Yellow, to Green like beans
and Red like a dragon's head,
to Blue like a baby's shoe!

25

Wow, how neat— Papa came to Tinsel Town
to meet a pretty famous athlete!

He set-up his lights and cameras when he realized something on his feet —

"Oh No, how could it be so?!"
Papa stepped on poop and jumped
Whoop, Whoop, Whoop!
At fault, was a tiny little Malt.

Number 2 had glued to his shoe;
he knew when the interview was
through—he had to get a tissue.
It was only a matter of time,
before the NEWS would swirl
and heads would twirl!

27

Papa was in his pajamas when he got the llamada, that he was off to the Bahamas!

Could it be true... PIGS were swimming in the deep blue?
Oink, Oink, Oink— Honks the tonk of the Pigs!

It was the NEWS of the day, the PIGS were here to stay!

28

On Y2K, pigs were sent to have a vacay,
but they embraced their nesting place,
so cut to the chase— Exuma is their new base!

They love to be graced by your pretty human face...
In fact, they are always ready for a selfie!

Oops, I almost forgot!
If you feel outpaced as you get chased...
look the PIGS straight in the face
and raise your arms into space!

29

Papa goes a long way on BIG NEWS days,
sometimes he's gone forever and a day...
Which makes Lala sad, when he misses their play dates.

NEWS

But when he comes home—
he goes: Beep! Beep! Beep!
"Make way on the freeway!
I have to go home and play with my little babe."

BEEP

MIAMI

BEEP

It's strange to say, but in an odd way
Lala is used to waiting night and day,
to steal her Papa away!

Oh Yay— Papa's here to stay!

Until...
Papa was at the casa, for less than a semana, when...

Ring.. Ring..
Sounds the phone when it sings.
Extra! Extra!
There is NEWS!
That's Papa's cue, to
pack his shoes and chase the clues.

Lala and Papa's adventures abound,
so stick around
and we will have you spellbound —
See You Around!

Photograph Courtesy of Leonardo Holanda

Meet Carlos & Lauren Rigau.

This is the true story of Carlos Rigau, a News PhotoJournalist and his adventures chasing news stories around the world throughout nearly forty years. Carlos' eye has seen the good, the bad and the ugly... Literally!

From civil unrest and riots to interviewing Presidents and Prime Ministers, Carlos has captured it all. The array of notoriety for his work, ranges from Emmy Awards to a Silver Angel Award... Along the way his eye has captured images that have touched the lives of so many.

From images of children crying and refugees fleeing oppression to the glory of the Athletic Games. To us the world is shown through the looking glass of our TV, on the other side of that glass, is a camera and what that camera has seen, inspired this book.

Along the way, Carlos had a baby girl, and just weeks after she was born, he was off to South Korea-- "So that is Papa's cue, to pack his shoes and go chase the clues..."

Growing up in a world bustling with Breaking News from the second she was born, Carlos's daughter LaLa, knew that writing about her father's adventures was the only solution.

After spending a year volunteering to teach children in low-income schools about the love of reading, LaLa was inspired to turn all of her Papa's memories into a Children's book!

LaLa hopes this book will inspire children to get to know the world around them, all the while understanding the responsibility of News gathering and those who gather it.

Before there were 140 Character stories... There were 140 steps taken to gather a story...
This is THAT story.

If you are not sure you know where to go, with some of those 'newsy' words...
Just find the time to climb inside and they will be defined!

Copyright © 2019 Lauren Rigau

All rights reserved. No part of this book may be reproduced in any form or by any electronic or mechanical means. Including information storage and retrieval systems, without permission in writing from the publisher, except by reviewers, who may quote brief passages in a review.

ISBN 9781097464166

Library of Congress Control Number 2019905699

Front cover image by AnnMarie Rapach

Some characters and events in this book are fictitious. Any similarities to real persons, living or dead, is coincidental and not intended by the author.

First Printing 2019

Visit www.TheAdventuresofLalaAndherPapa.com

Glossary

Abound (v) existing in great quantities or numbers

Adventure (n) an exciting experience

Bail of Hail (n) [*phrase*] bail: a container; hail: small lumps of ice that sometimes fall from clouds during storms

Beet (n) a leafy plant with a thick, juicy root, usually in a deep red color that is eaten as a veggie

Breeding (n) to procreate: producing an offspring

Camera Man (n) a person who operates a camera and makes it their business to take pictures
[ex: *photographer like papa*]

Casa (n) [Spanish] home or house

Command (v) the ability to control a situation: the power to give an order

Conceit (n) to create an elaborate image or far-fetched comparison

Cone (n) context: geometry- to make cone shaped [ex: *the cone of bad weather will be 3 miles long*]

Country [*con-trEE*] (n) an area of land that is controlled by its own government
[spelling: *Country*] [ex: *USA, Canada, England*]

Cue (n) [sounds like: *Q*] a signal to a performer to begin a specific action [ex: *lights, camera, action*]

Defeat (v) [*d-feet*] to win a victory over

Drone (n) [*dur-own*] unmanned aircraft that can navigate and take pictures without human on board

Edits (v) to glue moving pictures together on a computer /video recordings cut and rearranged

Embraced (v) [*m-brace-d*] to accept [*something, someone*] gladly

Gas Particles [*-charged+*] 1 of the 4 fundamental states of matter: solid, liquid, plasma, gas.
Found between liquid and plasma states of matter - gas is difficult to observe,
described via: pressure, volume, number of particles and temperature.

Grip (v) TV production technician who carries equipment

Glossary

Interview (*n*) a meeting where information is obtained [*by a tv reporter*] from a person

Inventories [*in-ven-to-rees*] (*n*) a list of current material, information or product which is stored as back-up

Llamada (*n*) [*spanish*] [*ya-ma-da*] a phone call

Malt [*Maltese*] (*n*) a breed of small dogs with a long silky white coat, black nose, dark eyes

News (*n*) a report of current events in a newspaper /newscast that can influence or effect people

Northern Lights (*n*) aurora borealis: broad bands of light that have magnetic and electric source.
    They appear in the night sky, especially in the Arctic regions

Ouï [*ew-eee*] 'yes' in French

Outpaced (*v*) to run or move faster than

Quest (*n*) [*k-west*] act of seeking - to make a journey in search of something
    [ex: *the family is going on a treasure quest*]

Rage (*n*) an intense feeling: passion

Scan (*v*) to look through or over something quickly

Scuffle (*v*) a short misunderstanding that is not very serious: to move very quickly with short steps

Semana (*n*) [*spanish*] the days of the week.. i.e: Monday [*Lunes*], Tuesday [*Martes*], Wednesday [*Miercoles*], Thursday [*Jueves*], Friday [*Viernes*], Saturday [*Sabado*], Sunday [*Domingo*]

Spell Bound (*adj*) enchanted, fascinated: holding one's attention as if you were bound by a spell

Stride (*v*) a way of walking or moving with long steps

Trillion (*n*) one million million 1,000,000,000,000,000,000

Tundra (*n*) a large area of flat land in the northern parts of the world, where the ground is always frozen

Y2K (*n*) the year 2000: y [*year*] + 2 + k [*thousand*] when it was thought there would be a worldwide
    computer outage

42680326R00024

Made in the USA
San Bernardino, CA
10 July 2019